Angels,
Archangels

*and All the Company
of Heaven*

Gottfried Knapp

Angels, Archangels

*and All the Company
of Heaven*

Prestel

MUNICH · LONDON · NEW YORK

Raphael. *Galatea*, 1511 (detail)
Palazzo della Farnesina, Rome (see plate 24)

Page 1:
Giambattista Tiepolo. *Allegory*, *c.* 1745. Museo Civico di Storia ed Arte, Triest

Frontispiece:
Raphael. *The Sistine Madonna*, *c.* 1513 (detail)
Gemäldegalerie Dresden. (see plate 25)

© 1999 by Prestel Verlag, Munich · London · New York
© of works illustrated by the artists, their heirs and assigns,
by VG Bild-Kunst, Bonn, 1999

Acknowledgments: p. 104

Translated from the German by Ian Robson
Copy-edited by Andrea P. A. Belloli

Prestel books are available worldwide.
Please contact your nearest bookseller or write to one
of the following Prestel offices for information concerning
your local distributor:

Mandlstrasse 26, D-80802 Munich, Germany; Tel. (89) 381 70 90; Fax (89) 381 170 935;
4 Bloomsbury Place, London WC 1A 2QA; Tel. (0171)323 5004; Fax (0171) 6368004;
and 16 West 22nd Street, New York, NY 10010, USA; TEL. (212) 627 81 99; Fax (212) 627 98 66

Typeset by Max Vornehm GmbH, Munich
Offset lithography by eurocom 4, Villorba, Italy
Printed and bound by Passavia Druckservice, Passau

ISBN 3-7913-2231-1

Contents

Pictures from the Other Side

Don't look now, but we are not alone: there's an angel flitting about on the page. I don't know if he is studiously following the words, or if indeed he can read, but at any rate he seems to be enjoying himself. When I started writing, he settled himself on the first line, chin in hand, wondering how this purported treatise on his species might develop. But he couldn't keep still for long. Soon he was swinging around on the arm of my desk lamp or ruffling my hair with the aerobatics he was doing just inches above my head. If I paused to think, he would land on the second hand of the clock or whiz round and round the pen I was holding, causing enormous doodles to appear on the page.

Angels are omnipresent. You rarely see them, but you can sense what they are doing. They make their presence felt whenever we use our imagination, whenever the power of reason reaches its limits. Angels do not necessarily resemble the image we have of them. The pictures we find in museums and on postcards represent the wishful thinking of artists of diverse periods and backgrounds; such depictions tell us more about human dreams than about the nature of celestial beings.

Angel, *twelfth century.*
Capital in Sainte-Madeleine, Vézelay.

The word "angel" readily comes to mind in connection with experiences and phenomena that defy rational explanation. With the aid of fabled winged messengers in human form, we attempt to humanize, domesticate, and make accessible to our own intellects that which is sent from "heaven", which would otherwise remain alien or even sinister. The angel is the personification of the numinous, the incomprehensible, the mysterious, and the mythic. In the course of human history, however, human beings have reacted in quite different ways to the supreme power angels embody.

Sitting at my desk, I am hardly likely to take it as a divine injunction or manifestation of angels if my hearing is suddenly assaulted by a blare of automobile horns from the street. But how might I have reacted if I had been a shepherd some two thousand years ago and seen the night sky filled with fiery clouds and flashes of lightning? What might we have heard from those mid-twentieth-century sighters of UFO's if they had lived in animistic societies or in medieval Christendom,

Facing page:
Raphael. Astronomy, *1508–9 (detail).*
Stanza della Segnatura,
Vatican Museums.

Peter Paul Rubens.
The Annunciation, *1620.*
Bozzetto *for a portion of the ceiling of Saint Charles Borromeo, Antwerp.*
Akademie der Bildenden Künste, Vienna.

instead of in the age of science fiction and space travel?

Thus, the study of angels is in fact the study of human beings, of the images we fashion for ourselves of the "other side", the world of spirits. The angels who cavort on cathedral portals and in our art galleries, who recline on tombstones, or who watch over sleeping children in attitudes of prayer are not creations of God but idealized likenesses of human beings. The "company of heaven" which is our subject here is thus in a sense very much of this world, behaving according to earthly laws and motivated by human emotions. And that is why angels are such a fascinating subject, moving us to sentimentality, awe— in some cases even to ecstasy.

Dreams of Flying

In all ancient cultures, winged beings were thought to act as couriers between this world and the next. This phenomenon must have had something to do with a particular human fascination or elemental longing. While human beings cannot exist without air, they cannot rise up into it by means of their own exertions. We need the earth — or water — to move from one place to another. Human beings have therefore always dreamed of being able to fly; this ability has always featured in important myths. If human beings could cast off their terrestrial fetters and overcome

Athena Fighting the
Giant Alcyoneus,
c. *180* B C.
East Frieze from the
Altar of Zeus at
Pergamon.
Pergamonmuseum,
Staatliche Museen
zu Berlin, Preussischer
Kulturbesitz.

Initiation into the
Rites of Dionysus,
50 B C.
Detail from a
wallpainting.
Villa dei
Misteri, Pompeii.

the force of gravity—perhaps with the aid of fire — they would no longer be captives of the earth. A person who can soar on wings above everyone else is akin to the gods.

Most of us have at one time or another dreamed that we stood on the edge of a very high cliff or at the top of a tower, lost our balance, and fell. — Then, shortly before waking, we began to fly. For the angels, this dream is a reality: they perch on the tops of cathedral spires, spread their wings, and glide gently down through the curling smoke from chimneys into the town. Even if they did nothing else for us but reenact this age-old dream of anxiety and longing, it would earn them a place in our affections.

Human beings have always sought to clothe what they thought to be the spirits of the air in human or animal form. Winged beings who mediate between the here and now and the realm of the gods and spirits, who are compatible with various states of existence, who bring tidings from transcendent spheres, are stock figures in the mythologies of nearly all great civilizations, and the dream of flying is more often than not associated with the same sorts of manifestations as are familiar from the Christian tradition. The flying deities and daemons of the Greeks are, as far as their job descriptions go, direct precursors of the company of Christian heaven. Hermes and Hecate, Iris and Niobe, the sirens and the sphinxes boasted such a comprehensive array of talents that they were equipped to discharge practically all the duties of an angel in the Christian cosmos. In some archetypal scenes, they demonstrate their characteristic poses and gestures with such convincing immediacy that in every detail they could have served as models for their successors.

Hermes or Mercury, the divine messenger of Greco-Roman antiquity, is the prototype for all such heralds of the Christian era; indeed, the Greek word for "messenger", *angelos*, was adopted as the generic designation for all the functionaries of the company of heaven. Hermes, the "angel" of Olympus, was the intermediary between creator and creation. He was the go-between, the bearer of glad and bad tidings; he had magical, ecstasy-inducing powers. Like the winged Hecate, he brought human beings together in fateful encounters and could ward off misfortune and bring happiness and prosperity; like Iris, he brought peace; and like Nike, he brought victory. He exploited the power of music, playing the lyre and — like the sirens — conjuring ethereal harmonies to escort the souls of the departed to the next world. Then there were the sphinxes and winged daemons of the Etruscans, guardians of the threshold between life and death, whose posts on sarcophagi or at the top of entrances to

Praxiteles. Hermes *(Roman copy),* c. 340 BC. *Archaeological Museum, Olympia.*

temples and mausoleums were later assumed by the angels of Christianity.

The biggest part in the shaping of our image of angels was played by the smallest of the winged deities of the Greeks, the naked archer Eros or Cupid. It was especially his most sentimental incarnation, that of the innocently mischievous cherub, that spawned a whole host of frolicking scamps to enrich the iconography of Western civilization. The Eros-child embodies the driving force to which he lent his name. He arouses basic instincts and stimulates the generative urge; his influence excites, irritates, enraptures; his poisoned arrowheads can engender festering wounds or bliss beyond compare.

Left: Pair of Erotes with Purple Cloaks, c. AD 330. *Fragment of a ceiling painting. Bischöfliches Dom- und Diözesanmuseum, Trier.*

Proclamation, Ecstasy

It was above all the artists of the Baroque age who showed us how much of this pagan sensuality had been carried over into the beatific workings of the Christian messengers of love. The most inspired visualization of erotic forces is not in fact a naked Greek urchin, but a half-clothed Catholic angel on an altar in Rome, who drives his burnished spear deep into the heart of a holy woman — the saint in question reported that, rather than excruciating pain, she felt burning desire. The architect and sculptor GIANLORENZO BERNINI's celebrated rendition of the ecstasy of Saint Teresa is an astoundingly explicit enshrinement in marble of the erotic — indeed blatantly sexual — undertones of a profoundly religious experience. The artist illuminated the Freudian dimensions of the saint's ecstatic vision, almost as if the mystic of Avila had vouchsafed her dream of lustful agony not to her confessor, but to a psychiatrist, who of course was immediately able to identify its phallic connotations.

Bernini's youthful angel with the ambiguous smile is reminiscent of Cupid in mythological love scenes. With his left hand he draws back the nun's habit to reveal his target; with the dart in his right hand he takes aim at the womb of the saint, who, with arms outspread, head thrown back, half-closed eyes, and open mouth, abandons herself to an only too earthly ecstasy. If visual art has ever succeeded in depicting the overwhelming power of eros, the arousal of sensual experience, and the "earth-moving" moment of sexual fulfilment, it was never done more convincingly than here. Nor has the academic world been slow to grasp the point. How many young art students have been enlightened by their lecturer's remark that "if Bernini is here portraying 'heavenly love', then I have known it too"?

Gianlorenzo Bernini.
The Ecstasy of Saint Teresa *(detail). 1644–7.*
Capella Cornaro, Santa Maria della Vittoria, Rome.

Giotto. The Annunciation, *1303–5.*
Arena Chapel, Padua.

The Assault

But it is not only in the wishful thinking of visionary saints that Eros rears his pretty little head. One of the essential themes of Christian iconography —the Annunciation—offers ample scope for erotic infusion, thus echoing the workings of the telekinetically generative god of antiquity. A winged presence enters a maiden's chamber by force, disconcerts her with words of wondrous praise, and shocks her with the bold assertion that she is pregnant, even though she is a virgin.

With this show-stopping entrance, with this announcement that a son of God is to be born, the archangel Gabriel would no doubt have been greeted with applause from Mount Olympus. But his mission was a good deal more portentous than either the picaresque intrigues of the ancient gods or the "good news" that the hero in a white hat imparts to the doe-eyed heroine of a modern soap opera or film. What God's envoy had to proclaim was nothing less than the begin-

Facing page:
Gianlorenzo Bernini.
The Ecstasy of Saint Teresa, *1644–7.*
Capella Cornaro,
Santa Maria della
Vittoria, Rome.

ning of a new age. Mary, in giving birth to Jesus, was laying the foundation for a new dispensation.

This abrupt launching of God's plan for human salvation, though tantamount to spiritual rape, can also be experienced as an event of touching intimacy. It certainly has been a greater source of inspiration for Western artists than any other story from the Bible. In the Arena Chapel in Padua at the beginning of the fourteenth century, GIOTTO once more conjured up the great cosmological pathos with which Byzantine artists before him had been wont to invest this scene. In the most prominent position in the chapel, on the face of the chancel arch, sits God the Father in majesty amid the thronging orders of angels. He charges Gabriel to visit Mary and initiate the miracle that is to establish the New Covenant. On the next level below, to the left of the sanctuary, the archangel kneels within an imposing Gothic frame and dispatches his message with outstretched hand over the top of the arch to the almost mirror-image space on the right, where Mary kneels with her arms folded to receive the heavy burden.

Giotto thus made masterly use of a psychological dynamic—the Western habit of reading from left to right—in order to dramatize his subject. The unseen message of the Annunciation follows the direction of a written text, thus effortlessly bridging the gaping void of the arch that separates the two protagonists. With his entirely logical organization of the elements of the composition, Giotto helps the viewer both to sense the importance of Gabriel's mission within the divine plan and to participate in the excitement and spirituality of the dialogue with Mary.

Lesser masters of the Gothic period, who were not quite so confident of their gift for pictorial composition, had found that a fluttering inscribed scroll would adequately convey the verbal message, usually running the words from left to right. If an artist did forgo the psychological effect of "reading motion", he must—as

Simone Martini. The Annunciation, 1333. Galleria degli Uffizi, Florence.

Burgundian Master. The Annunciation, c. 1450. Germanisches Nationalmuseum, Nuremberg

Matthias Grünewald did—have had a very good reason for doing so.

For the painters of the late Middle Ages and early Renaissance, the highly emotive encounter of envoy and handmaiden presented a great artistic challenge. No other subject provides as many clues to the temperament and imagination of artists. The handling of the space between the two figures is especially illuminating; it is often charged with a tense anticipation that can quite properly, if on a sublime level, be experienced as erotic.

When SIMONE MARTINI set the stately rhythm of three pointed arches against the motions of the figures below them, he was engaging in a very subtle exercise in sensuality. What could almost be described as an ardent longing draws the kneeling angel from the left "aisle" of the imagined church into the "nave", while Mary turns away into the right "aisle". The severe verticality of the tall lilies at the centre of the composition only serves to un-

derline the sensitivity with which the two bodies are made to react to one another with smoothly organic, parallel movements.

In the fifteenth century, the great painters used architectural elements more and more to enhance the expressiveness of intimate feelings. An ex-

ample is furnished by PIERO DELLA FRANCESCA's polyptych in Perugia, in which a vaulted colonnade in the middle of the picture disappears into such magical depths of perspective that it creates an almost bewildering vortex between Gabriel and Mary. FRA ANGELICO always set his

Annunciations in harmoniously protective, monastically bare spaces from which distracting attributes had been banished.

Beneath the softly contoured vaulting of a columned patio, his childlike protagonists perform the ritual of salutation with the innocence of brother and sister, as might be seemly for the eyes of the "brothers" and "sisters" of a religious institution.

It was only the young LEONARDO who liberated Mary from the hermetically sealed, antiseptic convent environment in which his colleagues had confined her and transposed the scene into the world at large, into the realm of Nature. The elongated horizontal format that broadens the scene in a literal sense in itself suggests a new outlook on the world. Here, a genius has torn down the walls of the Middle Ages and looked out over their ruins into the world beyond.

Leonardo's angel is a young nature god. He kneels in a luxuriant bed of flowers before the boldly contoured backdrop of a park, which opens onto a busy harbour in the distance. With a penetrating, almost procreative stare and a beseeching gesture of the hand, he dispatches his message along the long marble balustrade to Mary, a girl of shy yet inquisitive and knowing countenance, who stems the momentum of his words with a determined gesture of her own.

Leonardo here has shown us the clash of two forms of being, two creative principles. Where the angel, with naturalistic bird's wings, is the child of burgeoning nature, Mary is totally assimilated into the architecture that surrounds her, a majestic structure in the new Renaissance style, its huge door standing open at the right. The manly vigour of the angel, reflecting the inexorable course of nature, is thus contrasted with the static assuredness of Mary as described in the Scriptures. The creative force is expressed in terms of its transmitter and its receiver. Leonardo's statement is that Mary's body, so palpable under her robe, is to be the vessel for an elemental dictum issuing from distant spheres. The entrance into the new temple is through Mary's body. Without her, the splendid architecture of the New Convenant would have no point.

Leonardo da Vinci.
The Annunciation,
1472–5.
Galleria degli Uffizi,
Florence.

Rogier van der Weyden. The Annunciation, *1431. Musée du Louvre, Paris.*

Visits to a Young Lady's Chamber

The great Flemish painters of the same period used quite different means to conjure up the mystery of the Annunciation, staging the portentous transaction in a bourgeois parlour or bedchamber. ROGIER VAN DER WEYDEN, for instance, set the scene thus: on the left, by the hearth, is a bench with plumped-up cushions; on the right, a four-poster bed with neatly gathered draperies; against the back wall, an oak sideboard with a polished brass jug; and in the foreground, on the tiled floor, a blue china vase with white lilies. Amid these furnishings we see a young man dressed like an acolyte and a young lady whose attention to her reading has barely been interrupted by the arrival of her visitor. The fact that the latter has wings does not strike us as particularly unusual, any more than the pewter lamp hanging from the ceiling seems out of place.

Yet, for all the coolness of the two protagonists, something is in the air. The movements of their hands—and

Right: Matthias Grünewald. Virgin and Child with Angels, *Panel from the Isenheim Altarpiece, 1512–15. Musée d'Unterlinden, Colmar.*

eyes—make this obvious. These rhythms work on the beholder to imbue the consummately evoked "doll's house" setting with a depth of feeling that has few parallels in art. The neat little room, as brilliant a still life as one could hope to find, becomes part of a higher order of things, a stillness in which a miracle can occur.

Such a matter-of-fact ambience could also be used to stage high drama, as the ecstatic visionary GRÜNEWALD demonstrated in the left wing of the Isenheim Altarpiece.

He too depicted the chamber's furnishings with almost palpable realism, but in his work—and this is the astounding break with tradition—the angel explodes into the confined space from the right. The fulsome, shimmering plumage of his outspread wings practically shatters the doorframe, and the tail of his billowing red mantle shoots out like a flame toward Mary, who recoils in fright.

If we read this transposed, larger-than-life composition of the familiar scene from left to right, as we have become accustomed to doing, we no

longer follow the path taken by the blessing from its pronouncer, the angel, to its recipient, Mary, but experience the event in the passive, rather than the active, voice, through the eyes of a cowering girl. Through her we feel the inexorable supernatural force bearing down on us.

The transaction has suddenly become highly personal; indeed, it is made almost brutally evident that Mary's election will also involve suffering. There is no longer any hint of give and take between brother and sister, the erotically tinged play-acting of children which the Gothic painters showed us. This is a far cry, too, from the bourgeois propriety of the meeting in the neat and tidy bedchamber. With every detail, Grünewald makes it clear that this encounter marks the beginning of a drama involving human beings, which will bring to its personae not only the experience of bliss but also immeasurable sorrows. The *Annunciation* of the Isenheim Altarpiece is separated only by the thickness of a panel from the *Crucifixion*. When the wings of the altarpiece are closed, we are confronted with the ghastly spectacle of Christ's death, with the grief-stricken Mary swooning in the arms of Saint John. A scene that is elsewhere invested with youthful joyousness has thus been endowed with a depth of suffering that was not fully appreciated until the twentieth century.

With his unique visionary genius, Grünewald also sought to crystallize the Bible's rather vague and contradictory allusions to the nature and appearance of angels. Indeed, he is one of the few artists of modern times to have given any creative consideration to the concept of angels as spirits, not just as comely likenesses of human beings with wings on their shoulders. In the *Virgin and Child with Angels*, the centrepiece of the Isenheim Altarpiece, a fantastic array of spirit-entities has

been assembled to join the angelic consort in the left half of the picture. Behind the fair-haired youth playing the viola da gamba in the foreground, a fellow musician, a shimmering green nature daemon surreally bedecked with down and feathers, leans against the wall of the Gothic baldachin, itself a veritable jungle of rampant excrescences (see plate 10). Then comes a cavorting bunch of curiously dishevelled will-o'-the-wisps in glowing red balls, *cephaloptera* radiant with all the colours of the rainbow, and phosphorescent proto-daemons flickering up out of the dark. Then again, in the right half of the picture, high up above Mary, the broad expanse of sky is flecked with luminous clouds of swirling semi-transparent butterfly-spirits.

If art has ever succeeded in translating into visual terms the luminous and fiery essence of the heavenly hosts as described by the Old Testament prophets or Saint John in Revelation, then surely it must be here, in the cosmic kaleidoscope with which Grünewald framed the birth of Jesus. Christ's coming is the occasion for a new Creation, witnessed this time by a consummate visionary capable of cap-

Matthias Grünewald. The Nativity with Concert of Angels, Panel from the Isenheim Altarpiece, 1512–15. Musée d'Unterlinden, Colmar.

turing its myriad apparitions in form and colour. His account runs thus: in the beginning was fire; it proceeded from the Creator's throne in mighty flux toward earth; it diversified itself, and its flames assumed shapes; these were distilled into ethereal bodies, sprouted wings for independent motion, and gradually took on human traits.

Seraphim and Cherubim

These lucent elemental spirits, first seen by the prophets, later conventionalized as humanoid beings, and now portrayed by Grünewald once again in their archaic guise, originally comprised two species: the seraphim—fire spirits radiating an audible, incandescent aura—and the cherubim—incorporeal aerial entities, which with their three or more superimposed pairs of wings could hover like helicopters and were thus predestined for all static ministrations, such as eternal adoration around God's throne, sentry duty before closed gates, or the guarding of graves.

Albrecht Dürer. Festival of the Rose Garlands, *1506. Národní Galerie, Prague.*

Stefan Lochner. Angel Playing the Organ, c. *1430. Detail of* The Virgin of the Rose Bower. *Wallraf-Richartz-Museum, Cologne.*

Long after the church had decided that it was permissible for angels to look like human beings, the archaic varieties with only rudimentary torsos could still be found among the company of heaven. In STEFAN LOCHNER's view, for example, only the angel-musicians seated on stools could have their mantles filled out with anything like solid flesh. His puckish infants who, like shimmering blue humming birds, flit across the golden heavens are equipped with hands for praying but scantily endowed in the nether regions. Having no need for belts, their chemises tail off above what would have been their waists in daintily fluttering streamers.

Not even ALBRECHT DÜRER could bring himself to deny a share of the limelight to cute little mutations of the once-so-severe cherubim. On such an exalted occasion as the Festival of the Rose Garlands, the encounter between the representatives of contemporary society and the envoys of heaven is invested with an unexpected naturalism. Above Emperor Maximilian, the pope, Fugger (the picture's donor), and the other grandees of the day, the

Two Winged Angels, c. *1900. Postcard.*

The Handsome Winged Man

It was indeed a long way from the huge and intimidating headless creatures of earliest times, with their eye-besprinkled wings, to the marzipan dolls' heads of the Belle Epoque. Similar existential mutations over the centuries can be traced in representations of those members of the celestial hierarchy whom we know by name. Archangels are nowhere mentioned in written sources as having wings, nor did they appear with such appendages in visual representations until the fourth century A D. It was then that an anonymous mosaicist in the Church of Santa Pudenziana in Rome first

putti who float around the enthroned Virgin — in their bodilessness way behind contemporary thinking on angelic anatomy — are so disarmingly natural that the studiously arranged symbolic event could just as well be read as the record of an actual moment, a "group portrait with lady". Each merrily gesticulating putto pushes a tiny cloud with his chest, thus discreetly camouflaging the rest of his body.

In the nineteenth century, this sexless, chubby-cheeked stereotype with the winged shoulders conquered women's hearts, adorning albums and diaries in hundreds of sentimental poses. With their "impure" parts below the waist deftly removed and decorous cloudlets serving as bibs, cute little cherubs with clipped wings and touchingly outstretched pudgy arms obviously struck a chord of general sympathy. And, to gild the lily, there was the almost totally disembodied version, with soft down growing straight out of the truncated neck, like a ruff, and nothing in the rosy porcelain of the face to detract from the big, wide, heart-piercing eyes.

Saint Michael, *sixth century* A D. *Mosaic from San Apollinare in Classe, Ravenna.*

*Saint Demetrius,
eleventh century.
Kunstgewerbe-
museum, Staatliche
Museen zu Berlin,
Preussischer Kultur-
besitz.*

crossed the wingless, human-featured prototypes of the good angel with nameless bewinged, elemental spirits, thus creating (on the analogy of Greek models) the flying humanoid hybrid, possessed of worldly beauty and otherworldly faculties, that best corresponded to human ideas about a spiritual being between heaven and earth.

The handsome man with wings, whom we may regard as an archetype, was thus the creation of an artist. He was not the vision of an ecstatic prophet, nor was he invented by the church fathers as a figure worthy of emulation. Nevertheless, he has firmly implanted himself in our hearts. He has inspired dreams for a thousand years and more, and today, when so many people are searching for some kind of answer, he still serves as a pure and unimpeachable role model, romantic metaphor—or object of parody.

For the visual artists of the Byzantine world and early medieval Europe, who in their hieratic representations of the celestial orders still showed various classes of angels side by side, the anthropomorphic angel was a manly hero, a victor, a prince in magnificent ceremonial robes, who presided over the august rituals of the heavenly court with the dignity and panache of a major-domo. So, if we wish to study angels as executors of the Supreme Will and incarnations of universal wisdom, we need to look at Byzantine

The Madonna and
Child,
ninth century.
Apse mosaic from
Santa Maria in Dom-
nica, Rome.

mosaics and frescos or at Romanesque art, at the masterpieces of Ottonian book illumination, for example, in which gigantic angels watch over the workings of the world with wide-open, uncannily rolling eyes and unleash veritable tempests with the beating of their mighty wings. They possess such elemental grandeur that, in comparison, the hustle and bustle evoked in similar configurations by, say, Peter Paul Rubens begin to look faintly ridiculous.

The Dream of the
Three Magi,
twelfth century.
Cathedral of Saint-
Lazare, Autun.

When the Angels Learned to Smile

It was the Gothic age that first brought heavenly messengers down to earth; they became less aloof, more approachable in their new comeliness. Angels became almost like members of the family; they could serve to project decidedly worldly feelings and were capable of reacting like human beings and expressing their feelings.

The first major representative of this new generation is the curly-haired angel of the Annunciation on the west facade of Reims cathedral. His almost shy attempt at a smile changed the course of art. Such seductive charm, such inner joy emanates from his youthful physiognomy, and the angle of his head as he pronounces the solemn words is so eloquent, that several generations of cathedral sculptors were unable to dissociate the announcement of Christ's conception from this elusive smile.

Jan van Eyck. The Last Judgment, c. 1440. *The Metropolitan Museum of Art, New York*

Smiling Angel, c. 1250. *From the West Portal of the Cathedral of Notre Dame, Reims.*

The other principal context of angelic service in the Gothic period was Judgment Day.

The Bible makes only a few brief allusions to this spectacular event and craftily neglects to give a specific date. People in the Middle Ages nevertheless had a more detailed mental picture of the terrible day of reckoning, when the dead would be allocated to eternal bliss or torment, than of most other stories that the Bible relates in far greater detail. This is hardly surprising when we consider the grandiose horror-scenarios conjured up by artists all over Europe. The hosts of angels, which when arrayed as celestial hierarchies often seem to be little more than staffage, come into their own at the Last Judgment, when heaven and earth collide apocalyptically, and angels can show what they are made of, can demonstrate almost all of their faculties.

In the uppermost region, on each side of the throne of judgment, angels display the instruments of Christ's Passion. On the next level down, the giant trumpets have to be blown; the chilling fanfare causes the earth to quake, and the dead are jolted from their graves. The awful judgment drama, the segregation of good and evil, takes its inexorable course. The damned who have managed to escape the flames of hell must be pushed back into the claws of their tormentors. Here and there, angels and devils fight for possession of individuals still half buried in the earth. The blessed ones, who can still hardly believe their good fortune, must be assisted in the ascent to heaven's gate, where they are clad in splendid robes and welcomed by soft music. And midway between heaven and hell stands Michael, the celestial prince, the caster-out of Satan, with giant scales and sword assigning the appropriate fate to every soul.

The most dramatic visualization of this conflict is that on a slim panel by JAN VAN EYCK. Departing from convention, he placed heaven and hell not to right and left, but one above the other. The damned were now denied even a glimpse of the light of day; they fell directly from their graves into the infernal torture chamber below.

The huge figure of Death crouches with skeletal arms outstretched to seal off the nether world from that above it. On his back, striking an athletic pose with his mighty wings unfurled, Michael aims his sword at the monstrous skull, which—thrusting forward out of the picture's centre—hypnotically arrests the viewer's gaze.

Rogier van der Weyden. Saint Michael, *before 1450. Detail of* The Last Judgment Altarpiece. *Hôtel Dieu, Beaune.*

Music Class

That the angels should yearn for the
coming of Judgment Day and the
chance to perform their assigned func-
tions is quite understandable when we
look at the sort of routine duties to
which they were assigned by the
artists of the Gothic. Whether it be a
conference of the Holy Trinity, an as-
cension, a Coronation of the Virgin, a
reception for a saint, or an outpouring
of spirit, they are always packed together symmetrically in hierarchies,
ranks, or rings, heads turned mechani-
cally toward stage centre, as if they
had been wheeled in on cue from
backstage.

Occasions for joyful outbursts, or at
least contented smiles, these festive rituals might well be, but amid all this
stereotyped splendour none of the
artists quite managed to work such

Melozzo da Forlì.
Music-making Angel,
before 1481.
Detail of a fresco
cycle from SS Apostoli.
Vatican Museums.

Benozzo Gozzoli. Angelic Choir, *1459–61.*
Detail of The Journey of the Three Magi.
Palazzo Medici-Riccardi, Florence.

emotions into the angelic counte-
nances. If anything, their faces are
somewhat strained beneath their
weighty golden haloes, which like the
wheels of a locomotive rotate in parallel among the clouds. We sense little
of the jubilation that embraces the
whole of creation—and nothing of
the celestial harmonies that contemporary writings are full of.

This was a deficiency that had long
been felt. In ancient Greece, for example, the song of the sirens was sup-
posed to be bewitchingly beautiful, yet
the stone effigies of those temptresses
conveyed none of that beauty; an open
mouth alone did not produce music.
The Gothic painters, who wished to
create the impression of heaven as a

realm of sweetness and light, were well aware that the singing of angels could not be rendered with paint.

Some kind of remedy obviously had to be found. And so musical instruments, or at least sheets of music, were placed in the hands of the celestial extras. The angels, who had hitherto only emitted invisible seraphic tones, formed themselves into a mighty orchestra, and from then on the celestial spheres echoed with the sounds of fiddles and flutes, sackbuts and psalteries, harps and harmoniums. The most adept instrumentalists could be sure of a place in the foremost ranks, a few virtuosos were granted the use of a stool, and the player of the portative—a portable organ—had the privilege of sitting before God the Father to display his talents.

The painter-poets of the fifteenth century were masters of the art of touching the viewer's heart with their angelic musicians—often child prodigies who could scarcely get their chubby arms around the belly of a lute— and many other sentimental devices. The aptly named Fra Angelico had his angelic infants dance in a flowery meadow. BENOZZO GOZZOLI, in the *Journey of the Three Magi*, put them to work as gardeners, pruning roses, weaving garlands, and gathering herbs. MELOZZO DA FORLÌ instilled the familiar gestures of adoration and music-making with a powerful sensuality. All these very human touches furnish glimpses of paradise that are capable of moving even the most blasé twentieth-century viewer; these visions of heaven, however artificial their outward harmony may seem, are suffused with an intense lyricism.

The New Corporeality

Such works as these, in which medieval religious conceptions are elaborated with a new inspiration, also serve to demonstrate how radically, around the same time, the pioneers of the Renaissance were casting off the past as, looking to the models of antiquity, they sought to create a new image of the individual as an autonomous being. This fresh view of humanity also had consequences for the angels. The sexless aerobat who would not have raised an eyebrow behind convent walls was no longer called for. The angels of the new generation were quite conscious of their corporeality,

Sandro Botticelli. Zephyr and Chloris, c. 1485. Detail of The Birth of Venus. Galleria degli Uffizi, Florence.

Sandro Botticelli.
Cupid, c. 1485.
Detail of The Birth
of Venus.
Galleria degli Uffizi,
Florence.

cavorting impishly in the air above a naked baby Jesus by Albrecht Altdorfer or Lucas Cranach.

As early as 1439, on the *Cantoria* in Florence cathedral, DONATELLO had boldly appropriated the sensual energy of pagan antiquity for a Christian subject. The strapping putti—realistically modelled Florentine urchins—give vent to their celestial jubilation in a free-for-all dance; like the erotes of old, they unashamedly dedicate their fleshly vitality to the service of God.

In painting, SANDRO BOTTICELLI demonstrated how Christian and

indeed of their sexuality. And as they now had to share the stage with their naked ancestors, the winged gods and daemons of classical mythology, a new, sensual incarnation was soon found for them. The rediscovery of the boyish, nude Eros/Cupid furnished a model for the child-angel so beloved of the late Gothic age. Along with his drapery he cast off his inhibitions and cheekily displayed his private parts with all the naturalness in the world, no matter whether he was climbing into bed with Venus on a panel by Titian or DIEGO VELÁZQUEZ or

Donatello. Dancing Putti, 1433–9.
Detail of the Cantoria.
Museo dell' Opera del Duomo, Florence.

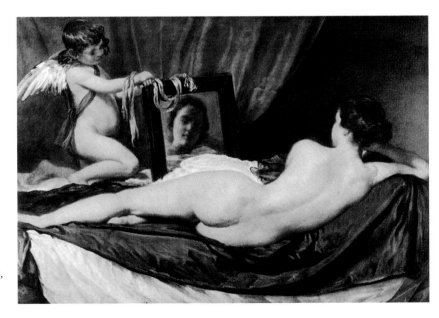

Diego Velázquez.
The Toilet of Venus
("The Rokeby Venus"),
c. 1650. National
Gallery, London.

Caravaggio. Triumphant Cupid, 1602.
Gemäldegalerie, Staatliche Museen zu
Berlin, Preussischer Kulturbesitz.

Gianlorenzo Bernini. Angel with the
Column of the Flagellation, *1669–70.*
Ponte Sant' Angelo, Rome.

mythological strata could be superimposed in one and the same picture. His Annunciation and Christmas angels would make accomplished courtiers in any nobleman's palace. Then again, the aerial spirits swooping in from the left in the *Birth of Venus* and the paunchy, blindfolded cupid who, in the artist's celebrated evocation of spring, aims his arrow at the Three Graces demonstrate aviatory techniques that would soon become the stock-in-trade of any self-respecting religious painter. In the hagiographic scenes of the Baroque, at any rate, exultant angels dive through the hallowed air with the same sort of diagonal aerobatics and just as much unabashed carnality as the inebriated acolytes of Silenus in the heady atmosphere of a mythological celebration.

Parmigianino.
Putto, c. 1532–5.
Detail from the Diana
and Actaeon cycle.
Rocca di Fontanellato.

Raphael. The Sistine Madonna,
c. *1513 (detail). Gemäldegalerie Dresden.*

Rosso Fiorentino. Madonna and Child
with Saints John the Baptist,
Anthony, Stephen, and Jerome, *1518.*
Galleria degli Uffizi, Florence.

Heavenly Seducers

A much more lasting impression was
made on the image of the angel in art
by another giant of the Renaissance,
who by both name and enduring popular affection would seem to have
been predestined for the angelic
sphere. In all phases of his short but
intense career, RAPHAEL produced
exemplary incarnations of members
of the celestial company. These were
canonized almost as soon as the last
touch of paint had been applied, were
idolized by succeeding generations,
and still constitute an inexhaustible
source of inspiration for copiers, com-
mentators, and caricaturists.

What is it that makes the two putti
in the *Sistine Madonna* so irresistible?
Is it the way they cast their eyes heav-
enward with puckish, inscrutable ex-
pressions, somewhere between yearn-
ing and yawning? Is it the dreamy,
pondering poses they have adopted
with childish coquetry? Or is it the
naughtiness of the Terrible Twins de-
clining to cavort appropriately among
the clouds and curtains, preferring to
loll about on the lower border of the
picture?

It is part of the sophisticated psy-
chology of this representation that the
protagonists, who are of human origin
and thus have no wings, float in the
air supported only by clouds, while
the two cherubs—who could fly if
they wanted to — rest on a relatively
stable ledge down below. The saints
are thus elevated to a more exalted
sphere, and the angels captured within
a very human dimension. The curtain
swings back to reveal the Virgin and
Child — a commanding, dynamic
moment. For all the theatricality, however, there remains a hint of the hap-
hazard, the banal, in this rendezvous
with the patron saints of Piacenza.
Saint Barbara does not appear to be
overly impressed by the awesomeness
of the moment; she does not look

upward to the resplendent majesty of Mary and the Apollonian infant Jesus, but downward with an almost enamored expression to the two little nude spectators with the chubby cheeks and irresistible smiles.

With the artful demeanour of the cherubs, Raphael imbued a subject offering little in the way of theological or compositional potential with human appeal, providing a whimsical foil to the symmetry of the conventional pyramid of saints.

The *sacra conversazione* had been a popular genre with patrons since about 1470. In such compositions, the holy men and women often just stand around looking bored, evidently unable to think of anything to say, and the atmosphere is often more suggestive of enervation than of conversation. To liven up these gatherings, artists often added a few baby angels merrily engaged in music-making, placing them approximately at eye-level for the faithful who would view the altarpieces. The masters of the genre openly competed over a period of several decades to see who could produce the most exquisite angels. If a modern art-lover had to award the victor's laurels, he would be hard put

to choose between the Venetians — GIOVANNI BELLINI, Vittore Carpaccio or Cima da Conegliano — and Raphael or his diligent disciples in Florence, Pontormo (see plate 19) and ROSSO FIORENTINO.

We must not only associate RAPHAEL with engaging little cherubs, however. Let us consider, for example, such a grandiose vision as the *Freeing of Saint Peter* in the Vatican apartments. Here, behind a martial grid of prison bars, we witness an explosion of light that invests the mighty winged champion who stoops over the apostle with a dazzling aureole and casts ghostly glints on the armour of the guards. Few visions have anticipated the spectacular Baroque fusings of space and light so consummately as this dramatic mystery play, which almost renders palpable the wall-shattering power of the celestial emissary.

Caravaggio.
The Seven Works of
Mercy, *1606–7.*
Chiesa del Pio Monte
della Misericordia,
Naples.

profusion of garland-swinging, flower-strewing angelic recruits.

It was the eruptive geniuses like RUBENS, conscious of their reputations as masters of dramatic effect, who were most susceptible to *horror vacui* and who found a remedy for it in massive accumulations of angelic extras, which, however, contributed more dead weight than dynamism to their compositions. Then again, in *The Fall of the Rebel Angels* and in paintings of the Last Judgment, whose *raison d'être* was the plummeting of bodies through the air, the specific faculty of winged flight had become largely superfluous.

Stupendous Baroque effects were produced not by anonymous heavenly hosts, but by the impingement of individual angels on the real world. CARAVAGGIO has left us some unforgettable examples. Whether his winged messengers watch over the Seven Works of Mercy or hand the palm of martyrdom to Saint Matthew as he lies stricken amid the murderous

Peter Paul Rubens. The Fall of the Rebel
Angels, *1623. Alte Pinakothek, Munich.*

Dance Troupes, Attack Squadrons

In the Baroque age — in the Catholic world at least — the story of salvation as depicted in churches entered the realm of grand opera. Angels appeared in every conceivable situation, but now they were often relegated to merely decorative roles, filling out compositions much like the ballet dancers in the mythologically based musical entertainments of the day. Ballet, indeed, is what comes most readily to mind when we contemplate the swirling patterns of angels in the works of Italian, Flemish, French, and Spanish painters of the Baroque era. Every available space is filled with a

Guido Reni.
Saint Michael, 1635.
Chiesa dei Cappuccini, Rome.

Rembrandt van Rijn.
The Angel Leaving Tobias and his Family, *1637.*
Musée du Louvre, Paris.

Caravaggio. The Rest on the Flight
into Egypt, *c. 1595.*
Galleria Doria Pamphilj, Rome.

tumult — however contrived the inter-
vention, the dramatic entrance of the
angel and the startling, impetuous
spontaneity of the keenly observed
gestures transform mundane events into cosmic happenings. The beguiling
cherub with the violin who plays to
Mary and Joseph in the *Rest on the
Flight into Egypt*, and the lascivious,
naked *amor vittorioso*, who unashamedly displays the still life between his legs, are creations by Caravaggio that stand out among the
masses of routinely churned-out
cherubs and cupids of the Baroque
period.

   In the Protestant Netherlands, however, the heavenly hosts were on the
retreat in the seventeenth century. The
sky above Bethlehem or Gethsemane
was no longer filled with carolling
choirs or hovering mourners, but was
once again the province of natural
phenomena. When, however, Rembrandt endowed with human feelings
the angelic apparitions recorded in the

Old Testament, he created some of the most moving of pictorial narratives. His angels are more like friends and helpers or, again, like invincible adversaries. Where Caravaggio's angel of inspiration swoops aggressively down on Saint Matthew like an arrow, Rembrandt's stands behind the pondering evangelist and whispers encouraging words in his ear — creating, indeed, a most appealing visualization of the Muse's kiss.

And REMBRANDT conjured up other unforgettable moments. Jacob wrestles doggedly with an opponent who holds him in an almost loving embrace. The healed Tobias and his family only begin to realize that they have received a boon from heaven when the friendly visitor soars mightily into the air before their eyes. And the aged Abraham, holding down the naked body of his son on the sacrificial pyre, is almost torn apart by the conflict of emotions he experiences when the youthful angel strikes the knife from his hand.

Ignaz Günther. Angel, 1752–3. Detail of the High Altar, Parish Church, Koprivná, northern Moravia.

Child's Work, Child's Play

In the eighteenth century, the gates of heaven were once again thrown open to all manner of winged creatures. Now everyone wanted their ceiling, dome, or vault embellished with cosmic spectacles, and this in itself created countless job opportunities for those with aerial skills. A new tactic of deployment also evolved out of the necessity to deal with large surface expanses. Fresco painters realized that the ceiling of a church or hall did not have to have every square inch packed with scenic activity, indeed that pockets of air between the focal points of attention could greatly benefit a composition. Allowing a tableau to breathe and come to life set off the actors to best advantage.

Angels were permitted to indulge their passion for exercise one last time on the expansive ceilings of Rococo churches. And, since such geniuses as Tiepolo (see plates 42, 43) managed to suffuse even their panel paintings with

Gianantonio and Francesco Guardi. The Wedding of Tobias, 1750–2. Chiesa dell' Angelo Raffaele, Venice.

Far left:
Joseph Anton Feicht-
mayr. The Honey-
Slaker, c. *1750.*
Detail of the Saint
Bernard Altarpiece.
Monastery Church,
Birnau.

Left:
Egid Quirin Asam.
Angel, c. *1738.*
Saint John Nepomuk,
Munich.

Martin Knoller.
The Resurrection,
1771.
Benedictine Abbey
Church, Neresheim.

this broad new airiness, the eighteenth
century has bequeathed to us a large
number of vivid and compelling angelic constellations.

A possibly surprising aspect of this
last great flowering of religious senti-
ment in art is the fact that sculptors
were, if anything, more heavily in-
volved than painters. In southern Germany, especially, it seems that church-
goers now craved tactile sensations,
three-dimensional figures of a readily
appreciable plasticity. So, once again,
the angels came to the rescue. Descending from the painted altarpieces,
they positioned themselves wherever
they might be useful or at least pro-
vide a decorative touch. They held
candles aloft, hung festoons, and drew
back curtains; they opened holy books
and trampled writhing serpents; they
carried instruments of torture and
shoved clouds about; they strained under the weight of tabernacles, picture
frames, and pulpit-baldachins and ex-
ercised their musical talents on rere-
doses, organ cases, and choir stalls.

Of the many whimsical, folksy masterpieces of southern German Rococo
sculpture, we can mention only one:

Annunciation's timeless message to a daintily posturing angel fashionably clad in a short chemise without suffering a loss of artistic credibility. Elsewhere, however, the twilight of the angels had begun long since. The Age of Enlightenment had no use for supernatural intermediaries; the winged herald from on high was reduced to little more than a tinsel decoration on a Christmas tree, to be taken down on Epiphany and packed away.

But that is not quite the end of our story. Though on the face of it, they had outlived their usefulness, angels refused to lie down and die. The rational intellect was evidently still conscious of irrational, unfathomable realities and was unable to dispense with poetic visions. Having served for centuries as one of the pillars of an official cosmology, the incarnation of spiritual powers began to play a role in a more private world of individual mythologies; the company of heaven was no longer made up of ministers of an exclusively divine will.

Ignaz Günther.
The Annunciation,
1764.
Former Augustinian
Monastery Church of
Saints Peter and Paul,
Weyarn.

the *Honey-Slaker* by JOSEF ANTON FEICHTMAYR. This Swabian remake of that ancient honey-lover Cupid stands in a corner of the shrine at Birnau, finger in mouth, relishing the sweet fruits of his thievery and brazenly displaying his naked charms for the delectation of pilgrims. In this ecclesiastical setting, we are not shown the bees' revenge or Venus's upbraidings, but the out-and-out profanity of the escapade brings home to us how closely related the nude cherubs of the church are to their pagan counterparts; indeed, in this late phase they are scarcely distinguishable from the acolytes of carnal rites. Clearly, we have arrived at a turning point.

Toward the end of the eighteenth century, it was still possible for an artist like IGNAZ GÜNTHER in Munich to entrust the delivery of the

Johann Georg Dirr. Putto, 1770–9.
Cathedral, Salem.

Winged Messengers

Around 1800 and again around 1900, *fin de siècle* dreams and anxieties may well have accounted for the greater prominence of anthropomorphic spirits than in the intervening years of what was, by and large, a materialistic, down-to-earth century. At the one end we have William Blake's visions of angels and the Devil, enshrined in both literary and pictorial form, or the winged child-spirits in PHILIPP OTTO RUNGE's romantic allegory *The Large Morning*; at the other, we have the mystical apparitions of the Symbolists, the wistful angels and shadowy chimeras with which Odilon Redon and GUSTAVE MOREAU figured the human soul. "Angels" appeared in a variety of situations, as the antithesis of satanic powers or as poetic metaphors for spiritual revelation, for the beautiful and the intangible, the weird and the wonderful.

When Marc Chagall peopled the wintry sky over his native Vitebsk with lovers and angels, when Paul Klee gave an inexorably present but invisible antagonist a face, or when Max Ernst designated as *Fireside Angel* a raging sky-borne monster of shreds and patches, they were employing what one could almost call literary devices to conjure up the uncanny; a subtly numinous element still pervades these heterogeneous visualizations, but the religious origins of the angel concept — and much more so its ecclesiastical connotations — now seem to belong to a dim and distant past.

Philipp Otto Runge. The Large Morning, *1803–10 (detail). Kunsthalle, Hamburg.*

Gustave Moreau.
The Angel of Sodom,
c. 1885.
Musée Gustave
Moreau, Paris.

Going to the Dogs

Since the middle of the nineteenth century, the relative paucity of artistically inspired depictions of angels had been offset by a veritable flood of popular sentimental versions. The benevolent spirits were brought down to earth, away from their cosmic ministry in the service of God, and put to work in human service as guards and menials. Where they had once flown through solid brick walls with ease, they were now obliged to use the tradesmen's entrance. They were still to be seen in thousands of cheap, glossy reproductions, desperately striving to keep benign smiles on their faces, wherever a protective hand was required to prevent a cute little child from toddling over the edge of an abyss or falling from a perilous perch on a rickety bridge above a foaming torrent.

For those who found this sort of thing a bit beneath their dignity, practically the only alternative was cemetery duty. This was also hardly an alluring prospect, to be frozen into some maudlin pose of mourning or humility and planted on top of a gravestone. It was indeed a dog's life, being at everyone's beck and call — to have occupied a place of honour among the exalted company surrounding the throne of heaven and to be reduced to something like a jester at the funeral court of some trumped-up factory-owner.

The angel's secular cousins, the genii and amoretti, were not faring much better in the salons of the Belle Epoque. With an affected dalliance harking back to the style of the Rococo painter François Boucher (see plate 49), they scattered roses into the *décolletages* of the would-be Pompadours who sat for portraits, or entwined decorative ribbons around voluptuous reclining Venuses. But in the face of stiff competition from flesh-and-blood dancing-girls who — at least on the posters of the day — were able to perform amazing feats of acrobatics in mid-air, the winged revellers who flitted their traditional ways across the walls and ceilings of urban mansions were soon mere shadows of their former selves.

Cemetery Angel. *Cimitero di Staglieno, Genua.*

The Kids Next Door

Curiously enough, it was the strait-laced Victorians in England who made the most remarkable contribution to the late nineteenth-century celebration of the worldly angel. The Pre-Raphaelites had paved the way by putting wings on their pretty models and thus creating an ideal of woman as an angel of virginal purity, yet with an erotic substrate strong enough to make her a welcome bedmate. Succeeding generations of artists found this sophisticated image very much to their taste. Pale, fair-haired, nebulous, elfin, with deep-set blue eyes, tapering chin, and wickedly pouting mouth set like a plump little cushion directly beneath a long, slender nose, this carnal angel differed from the winsome heroines of other pictures only by virtue of her fleecy, body-length wings. To our eyes, these ungainly appendages might appear to have been salvaged from a box of props; they look positively ridiculous against the slim, girlish bodies that are otherwise depicted with such naturalistic precision. In standing poses these wings are punctiliously extended, like the little finger of the hand that holds a teacup; in flight, however, they are quite illogically retracted flat on the back. Cousin Cupid is not much of an aviator, either: like a Victorian rent-boy, he wallows in his feathered finery as on an air mattress.

The sight of these members of some heavenly amateur theatrical troupe will no doubt prompt questions that the reader has been longing to ask for some time. How does one fly with such wings? Where do these puny creatures find the strength to lift their bodies off the ground? Where are the powerful muscles? And how do the angel-girls squeeze the masses of feathers through the narrow slits in the back of their school uniforms?

Out of the ethereal being of a remote sphere, the Victorians had produced the boy or girl next door, an attractive creature ideal for the projection of sentimental feelings. The myth had become just another fairy-tale, a piece of pulp fiction even. It is hardly surprising that the angels, having fallen so far from their first estate, should have kept a low profile in art during much of the twentieth century.

Adolphe-William Bouguereau. Young Girl Resisting Cupid, c. *1880. North Carolina Museum of Art, Wilmington.*

Down to Earth

And yet, so long as human capacity for wonderment is not completely extinguished, the agents of wonder will not forsake us. They are not going to surprise us with a brand new image; but in the familiar guises that have evolved over the centuries, we will continue to encounter them at the cinema, amid the bright lights of Soho or Montmartre, or pointing the way to the cashdesk when we do our Christmas shopping. We all have our own ideas of what they look like. Some may see them as naked little cherubs with beguilingly roguish smiles; others, equating the word "angel"

Veit Stoss.
The Annunciation,
1517–18.
Saint Lawrence,
Nuremberg.

Veit Stoss. Angel's Head.
Detail of The Annunciation, *1517-18*

with "honey" or "baby", will visualize more feminine forms. Let us in closing once again conjure up the angel as superhuman, powerful, transcendental. The arbiter of life and death on the Judgment Pillar in the transept of Strasbourg cathedral, or the participant in the festive scene of the angelic salutation by VEIT STOSS in the choir of the Church of Saint Lawrence in Nuremberg — look at these, and you will recognize the stuff of angels! And when, in the darkness of the Scuola di San Rocco in Venice, the angel of the Annunciation bursts like a projectile into Mary's chamber, a shower of putti in his wake, you will positively shiver at the mighty wind they create.

In the Old Testament, things were not always so clear-cut. When, one night, the patriarch Jacob saw ethereal beings descending from heaven on a ladder, he was hard put to find adequate words to describe the experience. It is easier for us. We need only to visit museums and churches to sense the beating of angelic wings. We see the nimbus of light that emanates from the guardian of Christ's tomb in REMBRANDT's picture; we hear the marvellous music of the many celestial orchestras in fifteenth-century representations; together with the Munich urchin in Ignaz Günther's sculpture (see plate 46) we feel the handclasp of his guardian angel — and we know that angels exist!

Jacopo Tintoretto.
Four Angels Bringing the Cross
to Saint Peter, c. 1556 (detail).
Chiesa della Madonna dell'Orto,
Venice.

You remember the frolicsome little angel who kept me company as I was beginning to write? Well, perhaps I was too pedestrian, for he soon flew off in search of a more exciting pastime. But his kinfolk have been popping in repeatedly to see how the book was progressing. If you care to turn back to the flyleaf, you will notice that one of the winged company poked his nose a little too inquisitively into the printing press. And now, if you open the window, look out into the night sky, and listen very carefully, perhaps you will hear the fluttering of myriad pairs of tiny wings...

Rembrandt van Rijn.
The Resurrection,
1635–9.
Alte Pinakothek,
Munich.

And lo, as when, suffused by dawn, Mars glows ruddy through the thick vapours low in the west over the ocean floor, so to me appeared — may I see it again! — a light coming over the sea so swiftly that no flight is equal to its motion; from which when I had taken my eyes for a little in order to question my leader, I again saw it grow brighter and bigger. Then on each side of it appeared to me a something white, and from beneath it, little by little, came forth another whiteness. My master still said not a word, until the first whitenesses appeared as wings; then, when he clearly discerned the pilot, he cried, "Bend, bend your knees! Behold the angel of God! Clasp your hands: henceforth you shall see such ministers. Look how he scorns all human instruments, and will have no oar, nor other sail than his own wings between such distant shores; see how he holds them straight toward heaven, fanning the air with his eternal feathers that are not changed like mortal plumage." Then, as the divine bird came nearer and nearer to us, the brighter did he appear, so that close up my eyes could not endure him and I cast them down; and he came on to the shore with a vessel so swift and light that the water took in naught of it. At the stern stood the celestial steersman, such, that blessedness seemed to be inscribed upon him; and within sat more than a hundred spirits.

DANTE, *The Divine Comedy*, Purgatorio 1, canto 2

1   *Victory of Samothrace*, second century BC.

And the angel which I saw stand upon the sea and upon the earth
lifted up his hand to heaven, and sware by him that liveth for
ever and ever, who created heaven, and the things that therein
are, and the earth, and the things that therein are, and the sea,
and the things which are therein, that there should be time no
longer: but in the days of the voice of the seventh angel, when he
shall begin to sound, the mystery of God should be finished, as
he hath declared to his servants the prophets.

REVELATION 10:5–7

2   Reliquary in the form of a triptych, c. 1160 –70.

3   *The Annunciation to the Shepherds.* From the Pericope Book of Henry II, 1007–12.

4   Hugo van der Goes. The Portinari Altarpiece, 1475.

5   Van der Goes. *The Adoration of the Shepherds*.
    Detail of the Portinari Altarpiece.

7   Jan van Eyck.
    Angel of the Annunciation.
    Detail of the Ghent Altarpiece,
    c. 1432.

8   Hans Memling.
    Madonna with Two Angels, c. 1485.

9   Albrecht Dürer. *Lute-playing Angel.* Detail of *Festival of the Rose Garlands*, 1506.

10   Matthias Grünewald. *Angel.* Detail of *Virgin and Child with Angels*
     from the Isenheim Altarpiece, 1512–15.

11   Giotto. *The Ognissanti Madonna*, c. 1310 (detail).

12   Giotto. *The Ognissanti Madonna*.

Look how the floor of heaven
Is thick inlaid with patines of bright gold:
There's not the smallest orb which thou behold'st
But in his motion like an angel sings,
Still quiring to the young-eyed cherubins;
Such harmony is in immortal souls;
But whilst this muddy vesture of decay
Doth grossly close it in, we cannot hear it.

SHAKESPEARE, *The Merchant of Venice*, act 5, scene 2

15 Fra Angelico. *The Coronation of the Virgin, c.* 1435.

16 Fra Angelico. *The Coronation of the Virgin*, (detail).

17   Michelangelo, *Angel with Candlestick*, 1494–5.

18   Antonio Pollaiuolo. *Angel*, 1467.

19 Jacopo da Pontormo. *Angel of the Annunciation*, 1527–8.

20 Donatello. *The Cavalcanti Annunciation, c.* 1435.

21   Sandro Botticelli. *The Nativity, c.* 1500.

22   Filippino Lippi. *The Vision of Saint Bernard*, before 1480 (detail).

23   Sandro Botticelli.
*Zephyr
and Nymph*.
Detail
of *Primavera*,
c. 1478.

24   Raphael.
Galatea, 1511.

25 Raphael. *The Sistine Madonna, c.* 1513.

26 Raphael. *The Sistine Madonna* (detail).

27 Andrea del Verrocchio. *Putto and Dolphin, c.* 1470.

28 Titian. *The Education of Cupid, c.* 1565 (detail).

29 Titian. *The Annunciation, c.* 1566.

30 Bartolomé Esteban Murillo. *The Immaculate Conception,* 1678.

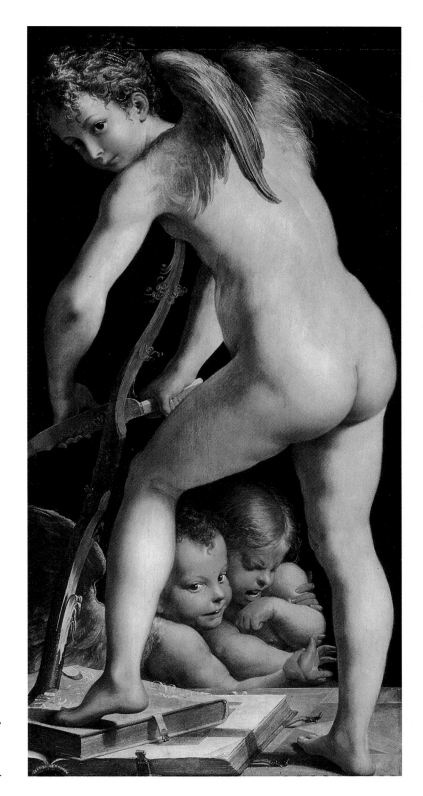

31 Bronzino.
An Allegory with
Venus and Cupid,
1544–5.

32 Parmigianino.
Amor, after 1531.

33 El Greco.
*The Assumption
of the Virgin,*
1607–13.

34 El Greco.
*The Assumption
of the Virgin*
(detail).

And when the tempter came to him, he said, If thou be the
Son of God, command that these stones be made bread.
But Jesus answered and said, It is written, Man shall not live
by bread alone, but by every word that proceedeth out of the
mouth of God.

MATTHEW 4:3–4

previous pages:

35   Correggio.
     Music-making Angels, c. 1526 (detail).

36   Tintoretto.
     The Annunciation, c. 1565–7.

37   Tintoretto.
     The Temptation of Christ, c. 1565–7.

And there was war in heaven: Michael and his angels fought against the dragon; and the dragon fought and his angels, and prevailed not; neither was their place found any more in heaven. And the great dragon was cast out, that old serpent, called the Devil, and Satan, which deceiveth the whole world: he was cast out into the earth, and his angels were cast out with him.

REVELATION 12:7–9

38 · Hubert Gerhard.
Saint Michael, 1588.

39 Peter Paul Rubens.
The Fall of the Rebel Angels, 1623.

40 Peter Paul Rubens and Jan Bruegel the Elder.
Madonna in a Garland of Flowers, c. 1620.

41 Rubens and Bruegel the Elder.
Madonna in a Garland of Flowers (detail).

42   Giambattista Tiepolo. *The Sacrifice of Isaac*, 1726–8.

43   Giambattista Tiepolo. *Apollo and the Horae*, 1752–3 (detail).

44   Joseph Christian. *The Resurrection of the Dead, c.* 1750.

45   Egid Quirin Asam. *The Assumption of the Virgin,c.* 1722.

He shall cover thee with his feathers, and under his wings
shalt thou trust: his truth be thy shield and buckler.

PSALM 91 : 4

46   Ignaz Günther. *Guardian Angel*, 1763.

47   Gottfried Bernhard Götz. *Music-making Angels*, 1749.

48 Etienne-Maurice Flaconet.
Cupid, 1757.

49 François Boucher.
The Rising of the Sun, 1753.

And at the midpoint, with outstretched wings, I saw more
than a thousand Angels making festival, each one distinct in
effulgence and in ministry. I saw there, smiling to their sports
and to their songs, a beauty which was gladness in the eyes of
all the other saints. And had I equal wealth in speech as in
conception, yet would I not dare to attempt the least of her
delightfulness.

DANTE, *The Divine Comedy,* Paradiso 1, canto 31

50   Antonio Canova. *Cupid and Psyche,* 1787–93.

51　Gustave Doré. *Dante and Beatrice in Eternity*, 1865.

Who, if I cried out, would heed me amid the host of the Angels?
Still, should an Angel exalt and fold me into his heart I should
vanish, lost in his greater being. For beauty is only a seed of
dread to be endured yet adored since it disdains to destroy us.
An Angel, alone, is misted in dread.

RAINER MARIA RILKE, *The Duino Elegies,* The First Elegy

52   Auguste Rodin.
The Fall of Icarus,
1896.

53   Adolphe-William
Bouguereau.
Cupid and Psyche,
1895.

The fair creature came towards us, clothed in white and such in his face as seems the tremulous morning star. He opened his arms and then spread his wings and said, "Come: the steps are at hand here, and henceforth the climb is easy".

DANTE, *The Divine Comedy,* Purgatorio 1, canto 12

54 Edward Burne-Jones. *Angel, c.* 1860.

55 Franz von Stuck. *The Guardian of Paradise,* 1889.